Speak Life
to the
NEXT GENERATION

A Journal for Families Everywhere

Annie Wimberly Rivers

Order this book online at www.trafford.com
or email orders@trafford.com

Most Trafford titles are also available at major online book retailers.

Scripture taken from the Holy Bible, New International Version.
Copyright ©1973, 1978, 1984 by International Bible Society. Used by permission of
Zondervan Publishing House. All rights reserved

Printed in the United States of America.

ISBN: 978-1-4669-2233-4 (sc)
ISBN: 978-1-4669-2232-7 (hc)
ISBN: 978-1-4669-2231-0 (e)

Library of Congress Control Number: 2012905594

Trafford rev. 04/27/2012

 www.trafford.com

North America & international
toll-free: 1 888 232 4444 (USA & Canada)
phone: 250 383 6864 ✦ fax: 812 355 4082

Tell it to your children, and let your children tell it to their children, and their children to the next generation.

—Joel 3:1 NIV

DEDICATION

This family journal is dedicated to families everywhere, especially my parents Creasey and Taylor, my children Crystal, Cherie, Deon and our next generation.

We will not hide them from the children; we will tell the next generation the praiseworthy deeds of the Lord, his power, and the wonders he has done. Psalm 78:4

INTRODUCTION

It is my hope that parents, grandparents, aunts, uncles, those serving in the military and friends of children and young people will speak life to the next generation. Consider this journal a tool for you to pass on encouragement, faith in God, and the many life experiences, principles and lessons that will help your young people to navigate the seasons of life, both positives and challenges. Journaling is an effective way to express, empower and embrace loved ones. Write from your heart about the things that matter most and how grateful and valuable they are to you, as well as the vision and dreams you have for them. Do this on a regular basis and, at the appropriate time, (e.g. graduations, birthdays, etc.) share as a special gift which I believe will be cherished for a life time.

The scriptures used are intended to encourage you, as you **Speak Life to the Next Generation!!!!**

THIS JOURNAL IS FOR

Name: _____

From: _____

Date: _____

Honor your father and your mother, so that you may live long in the land the Lord your God is giving you.

Exodus 20:12

_____

_____

_____

_____

_____

_____

_____

_____

_____

_____

Encourage the young person to be self-controlled.

Titus 2:6

_____

_____

_____

_____

_____

_____

_____

_____

_____

_____

_____

For I know the plans I have for you, "declares the Lord," plans to prosper you and not to harm you, plans to give you hope and a future.

Jeremiah 29:11

I praise you because I am fearfully and wonderfully made, your works are wonderful.

Psalm 139:14

_____

_____

_____

_____

_____

_____

_____

_____

_____

_____

_____

_____

Everyone must submit himself to the governing authorities, for there is no authority except that which God has established.

Romans 13:1

_____

_____

_____

_____

_____

_____

_____

_____

_____

_____

Trust in the Lord with all your heart and lean not on your own understanding; in all your ways acknowledge him, and he will direct your paths.

Proverbs 3:5-6

———————————————————————————

———————————————————————————

———————————————————————————

———————————————————————————

———————————————————————————

———————————————————————————

———————————————————————————

———————————————————————————

———————————————————————————

I can do all things through Christ who strengthens me.

Philippians 4:13

_____

_____

_____

_____

_____

_____

_____

_____

_____

_____

_____

All things work together for good to them that love God, to them who are called according to His purpose.

Romans 8:28

_____

_____

_____

_____

_____

_____

_____

_____

_____

_____

For God so loved the world that he gave his one and only son, that whoever believes in him shall not perish but have eternal life.

John 3:16

_____

_____

_____

_____

_____

_____

_____

_____

_____

_____

How can a young person stay pure? By obeying your word and following its rules.

Psalms 119:9

Love is patient, love is kind, it does not envy it does not boast, it is not proud. It is not rude, it is not self-seeking, it is not easily angered, it keeps no record of wrong.

I Corinthian 13:4-5

_____

_____

_____

_____

_____

_____

_____

_____

_____

How great is the love the Father has lavished on us, that we should be called children of God and that is what we are.

1 John 3:1

_____

_____

_____

_____

_____

_____

_____

_____

_____

_____

Fathers do not exasperate your children,
instead, bring them up in the training and
instruction of the Lord.

Ephesians 6:4

_____

_____

_____

_____

_____

_____

_____

_____

_____

_____

Honor your father and your mother, so that you may live long in the land the Lord your God is giving you.

Exodus 20:12

_____

_____

_____

_____

_____

_____

_____

_____

_____

Encourage the young person to be self-controlled.

Titus 2:6

For I know the plans I have for you, "declares the Lord," plans to prosper you and not to harm you, plans to give you hope and a future.

Jeremiah 29:11

_____

_____

_____

_____

_____

_____

_____

_____

_____

_____

I praise you because I am fearfully and wonderfully made, your works are wonderful.

Psalm 139:14

_____

_____

_____

_____

_____

_____

_____

_____

_____

_____

_____

Everyone must submit himself to the governing authorities, for there is no authority except that which God has established.

Romans 13:1

_____

_____

_____

_____

_____

_____

_____

_____

_____

_____

Trust in the Lord with all your heart and lean not on your own understanding; in all your ways acknowledge him, and he will direct your paths.

Proverbs 3:5-6

_____

_____

_____

_____

_____

_____

_____

_____

_____

_____

I can do all things through Christ who strengthens me.

Philippians 4:13

_____

_____

_____

_____

_____

_____

_____

_____

_____

_____

_____

All things work together for good to them that love God, to them who are called according to His purpose.

Romans 8:28

_____

_____

_____

_____

_____

_____

_____

_____

_____

For God so loved the world that he gave his one and only son, that whoever believes in him shall not perish but have eternal life.

John 3:16

_____

_____

_____

_____

_____

_____

_____

_____

_____

_____

_____

How can a young person stay pure? By obeying your word and following its rules.

Psalms 119:9

_____

_____

_____

_____

_____

_____

_____

_____

_____

_____

_____

Love is patient, love is kind, it does not envy it does not boast, it is not proud. It is not rude, it is not self-seeking, it is not easily angered, it keeps no record of wrong.

I Corinthian 13:4-5

_____

_____

_____

_____

_____

_____

_____

_____

_____

How great is the love the Father has lavished on us, that we should be called children of God and that is what we are.

1 John 3:1

_____

_____

_____

_____

_____

_____

_____

_____

_____

_____

Fathers do not exasperate your children, instead, bring them up in the training and instruction of the Lord.

Ephesians 6:4

_____

_____

_____

_____

_____

_____

_____

_____

_____

_____

Honor your father and your mother, so that you may live long in the land the Lord your God is giving you.

Exodus 20:12

_____

_____

_____

_____

_____

_____

_____

_____

_____

_____

Encourage the young person to be self-controlled.

Titus 2:6

_____

_____

_____

_____

_____

_____

_____

_____

_____

_____

_____

For I know the plans I have for you, "declares the Lord," plans to prosper you and not to harm you, plans to give you hope and a future.

Jeremiah 29:11

_____

_____

_____

_____

_____

_____

_____

_____

_____

_____

I praise you because I am fearfully and wonderfully made, your works are wonderful.

Psalm 139:14

Everyone must submit himself to the governing authorities, for there is no authority except that which God has established.

Romans 13:1

_____

_____

_____

_____

_____

_____

_____

_____

_____

_____

Trust in the Lord with all your heart and lean not on your own understanding; in all your ways acknowledge him, and he will direct your paths.

Proverbs 3:5-6

_____

_____

_____

_____

_____

_____

_____

_____

_____

I can do all things through Christ who strengthens me.

Philippians 4:13

All things work together for good to them that love God, to them who are called according to His purpose.

Romans 8:28

_____

_____

_____

_____

_____

_____

_____

_____

_____

_____

_____

For God so loved the world that he gave his one and only son, that whoever believes in him shall not perish but have eternal life.

John 3:16

_____

_____

_____

_____

_____

_____

_____

_____

_____

_____

How can a young person stay pure? By obeying your word and following its rules.

Psalms 119:9

_____

_____

_____

_____

_____

_____

_____

_____

_____

_____

_____

_____

Love is patient, love is kind, it does not envy it does not boast, it is not proud. It is not rude, it is not self-seeking, it is not easily angered, it keeps no record of wrong.

I Corinthian 13:4-5

_____

_____

_____

_____

_____

_____

_____

_____

_____

_____

How great is the love the Father has lavished on us, that we should be called children of God and that is what we are.

1 John 3:1

_____

_____

_____

_____

_____

_____

_____

_____

_____

_____

Fathers do not exasperate your children, instead, bring them up in the training and instruction of the Lord.

Ephesians 6:4

Honor your father and your mother, so that you may live long in the land the Lord your God is giving you.

Exodus 20:12

_____

_____

_____

_____

_____

_____

_____

_____

_____

_____

Encourage the young person to be self-controlled.

Titus 2:6

_____

_____

_____

_____

_____

_____

_____

_____

_____

_____

_____

For I know the plans I have for you, "declares the Lord," plans to prosper you and not to harm you, plans to give you hope and a future.

Jeremiah 29:11

_____

_____

_____

_____

_____

_____

_____

_____

_____

_____

I praise you because I am fearfully and wonderfully made, your works are wonderful.

Psalm 139:14

_____

_____

_____

_____

_____

_____

_____

_____

_____

_____

_____

Everyone must submit himself to the governing authorities, for there is no authority except that which God has established.

Romans 13:1

_____

_____

_____

_____

_____

_____

_____

_____

_____

_____

Trust in the Lord with all your heart and lean not on your own understanding; in all your ways acknowledge him, and he will direct your paths.

Proverbs 3:5-6

_____

_____

_____

_____

_____

_____

_____

_____

_____

_____

I can do all things through Christ who strengthens me.

Philippians 4:13

_____

_____

_____

_____

_____

_____

_____

_____

_____

_____

_____

_____

All things work together for good to them that love God, to them who are called according to His purpose.

Romans 8:28

_____

_____

_____

_____

_____

_____

_____

_____

_____

_____

For God so loved the world that he gave his one and only son, that whoever believes in him shall not perish but have eternal life.

John 3:16

_____

_____

_____

_____

_____

_____

_____

_____

_____

_____

How can a young person stay pure? By obeying your word and following its rules.

Psalms 119:9

_____

_____

_____

_____

_____

_____

_____

_____

_____

_____

_____

Love is patient, love is kind, it does not envy it does not boast, it is not proud. It is not rude, it is not self-seeking, it is not easily angered, it keeps no record of wrong.

I Corinthian 13:4-5

_____

_____

_____

_____

_____

_____

_____

_____

_____

How great is the love the Father has lavished on us, that we should be called children of God and that is what we are.

1 John 3:1

_____

_____

_____

_____

_____

_____

_____

_____

_____

_____

*Fathers do not exasperate your children,
instead, bring them up in the training and
instruction of the Lord.*

Ephesians 6:4

_____

_____

_____

_____

_____

_____

_____

_____

_____

_____

_____

Honor your father and your mother, so that you may live long in the land the Lord your God is giving you.

Exodus 20:12

_____

_____

_____

_____

_____

_____

_____

_____

_____

_____

Encourage the young person to be self-controlled.

Titus 2:6

_____

_____

_____

_____

_____

_____

_____

_____

_____

_____

_____

For I know the plans I have for you, "declares the Lord," plans to prosper you and not to harm you, plans to give you hope and a future.

Jeremiah 29:11

_____

_____

_____

_____

_____

_____

_____

_____

_____

_____

I praise you because I am fearfully and wonderfully made, your works are wonderful.

Psalm 139:14

_____

_____

_____

_____

_____

_____

_____

_____

_____

_____

_____

_____

Everyone must submit himself to the governing authorities, for there is no authority except that which God has established.

Romans 13:1

_____

_____

_____

_____

_____

_____

_____

_____

_____

_____

Trust in the Lord with all your heart and lean not on your own understanding; in all your ways acknowledge him, and he will direct your paths.

Proverbs 3:5-6

_____

_____

_____

_____

_____

_____

_____

_____

_____

I can do all things through Christ who strengthens me.

Philippians 4:13

_____

_____

_____

_____

_____

_____

_____

_____

_____

_____

_____

All things work together for good to them that love God, to them who are called according to His purpose.

Romans 8:28

_____

_____

_____

_____

_____

_____

_____

_____

_____

_____

For God so loved the world that he gave his one and only son, that whoever believes in him shall not perish but have eternal life.

John 3:16

_____

_____

_____

_____

_____

_____

_____

_____

_____

_____

How can a young person stay pure? By obeying your word and following its rules.

Psalms 119:9

_____

_____

_____

_____

_____

_____

_____

_____

_____

_____

Love is patient, love is kind, it does not envy it does not boast, it is not proud. It is not rude, it is not self-seeking, it is not easily angered, it keeps no record of wrong.

I Corinthian 13:4-5

_____

_____

_____

_____

_____

_____

_____

_____

_____

How great is the love the Father has lavished on us, that we should be called children of God and that is what we are.

1 John 3:1

Fathers do not exasperate your children, instead, bring them up in the training and instruction of the Lord.

Ephesians 6:4

Honor your father and your mother, so that you may live long in the land the Lord your God is giving you.

Exodus 20:12

_____

_____

_____

_____

_____

_____

_____

_____

_____

_____

_____

Encourage the young person to be self-controlled.

Titus 2:6

_____

_____

_____

_____

_____

_____

_____

_____

_____

_____

For I know the plans I have for you, "declares the Lord," plans to prosper you and not to harm you, plans to give you hope and a future.

Jeremiah 29:11

I praise you because I am fearfully and wonderfully made, your works are wonderful.

Psalm 139:14

_____

_____

_____

_____

_____

_____

_____

_____

_____

_____

Everyone must submit himself to the governing authorities, for there is no authority except that which God has established.

Romans 13:1

Trust in the Lord with all your heart and lean not on your own understanding; in all your ways acknowledge him, and he will direct your paths.

Proverbs 3:5-6

_____

_____

_____

_____

_____

_____

_____

_____

_____

I can do all things through Christ who strengthens me.

Philippians 4:13

_____

_____

_____

_____

_____

_____

_____

_____

_____

_____

_____

All things work together for good to them that love God, to them who are called according to His purpose.

Romans 8:28

_____

_____

_____

_____

_____

_____

_____

_____

_____

_____

For God so loved the world that he gave his one and only son, that whoever believes in him shall not perish but have eternal life.

John 3:16

How can a young person stay pure? By obeying your word and following its rules.

Psalms 119:9

_____

_____

_____

_____

_____

_____

_____

_____

_____

_____

_____

Love is patient, love is kind, it does not envy it does not boast, it is not proud. It is not rude, it is not self-seeking, it is not easily angered, it keeps no record of wrong.

I Corinthian 13:4-5

How great is the love the Father has lavished on us, that we should be called children of God and that is what we are.

1 John 3:1

_____

_____

_____

_____

_____

_____

_____

_____

_____

Fathers do not exasperate your children, instead, bring them up in the training and instruction of the Lord.

Ephesians 6:4

Honor your father and your mother, so that you may live long in the land the Lord your God is giving you.

Exodus 20:12

_____

_____

_____

_____

_____

_____

_____

_____

_____

_____

Encourage the young person to be self-controlled.

Titus 2:6

_____

_____

_____

_____

_____

_____

_____

_____

_____

_____

_____

_____

For I know the plans I have for you, "declares the Lord," plans to prosper you and not to harm you, plans to give you hope and a future.

Jeremiah 29:11

_____

_____

_____

_____

_____

_____

_____

_____

_____

I praise you because I am fearfully and wonderfully made, your works are wonderful.

Psalm 139:14

_____

_____

_____

_____

_____

_____

_____

_____

_____

_____

_____

_____

Everyone must submit himself to the governing authorities, for there is no authority except that which God has established.

Romans 13:1

_____

_____

_____

_____

_____

_____

_____

_____

_____

_____

_____

Trust in the Lord with all your heart and lean not on your own understanding; in all your ways acknowledge him, and he will direct your paths.

Proverbs 3:5-6

_____

_____

_____

_____

_____

_____

_____

_____

_____

I can do all things through Christ who strengthens me.

Philippians 4:13

All things work together for good to them that love God, to them who are called according to His purpose.

Romans 8:28

_____

_____

_____

_____

_____

_____

_____

_____

_____

For God so loved the world that he gave his one and only son, that whoever believes in him shall not perish but have eternal life.

John 3:16

_____

_____

_____

_____

_____

_____

_____

_____

_____

How can a young person stay pure? By obeying your word and following its rules.

Psalms 119:9

Love is patient, love is kind, it does not envy it does not boast, it is not proud. It is not rude, it is not self-seeking, it is not easily angered, it keeps no record of wrong.

I Corinthian 13:4-5

_____

_____

_____

_____

_____

_____

_____

_____

_____

How great is the love the Father has lavished on us, that we should be called children of God and that is what we are.

1 John 3:1

_____

_____

_____

_____

_____

_____

_____

_____

_____

_____

Fathers do not exasperate your children, instead, bring them up in the training and instruction of the Lord.

Ephesians 6:4

Honor your father and your mother, so that you may live long in the land the Lord your God is giving you.

Exodus 20:12

_____

_____

_____

_____

_____

_____

_____

_____

_____

Encourage the young person to be self-controlled.

Titus 2:6

For I know the plans I have for you, "declares the Lord," plans to prosper you and not to harm you, plans to give you hope and a future.

Jeremiah 29:11

I praise you because I am fearfully and wonderfully made, your works are wonderful.

Psalm 139:14

Everyone must submit himself to the governing authorities, for there is no authority except that which God has established.

Romans 13:1

_____

_____

_____

_____

_____

_____

_____

_____

_____

Trust in the Lord with all your heart and lean not on your own understanding; in all your ways acknowledge him, and he will direct your paths.

Proverbs 3:5-6

_____

_____

_____

_____

_____

_____

_____

_____

I can do all things through Christ who strengthens me.

Philippians 4:13

_____

_____

_____

_____

_____

_____

_____

_____

_____

_____

All things work together for good to them that love God, to them who are called according to His purpose.

Romans 8:28

_____

_____

_____

_____

_____

_____

_____

_____

_____

_____

For God so loved the world that he gave his one and only son, that whoever believes in him shall not perish but have eternal life.

John 3:16

_____

_____

_____

_____

_____

_____

_____

_____

_____

_____

*How can a young person stay pure? By obeying
your word and following its rules.*

Psalms 119:9

_____

_____

_____

_____

_____

_____

_____

_____

_____

_____

_____

Love is patient, love is kind, it does not envy it does not boast, it is not proud. It is not rude, it is not self-seeking, it is not easily angered, it keeps no record of wrong.

I Corinthian 13:4-5

_____

_____

_____

_____

_____

_____

_____

_____

_____

How great is the love the Father has lavished on us, that we should be called children of God and that is what we are.

1 John 3:1

Fathers do not exasperate your children, instead, bring them up in the training and instruction of the Lord.

Ephesians 6:4

_____

_____

_____

_____

_____

_____

_____

_____

_____

_____

Honor your father and your mother, so that you may live long in the land the Lord your God is giving you.

Exodus 20:12

_____

_____

_____

_____

_____

_____

_____

_____

_____

Encourage the young person to be self-controlled.

Titus 2:6

_____

_____

_____

_____

_____

_____

_____

_____

_____

_____

_____

For I know the plans I have for you, "declares the Lord," plans to prosper you and not to harm you, plans to give you hope and a future.

Jeremiah 29:11

I praise you because I am fearfully and wonderfully made, your works are wonderful.

Psalm 139:14

_____

_____

_____

_____

_____

_____

_____

_____

_____

_____

_____

Everyone must submit himself to the governing authorities, for there is no authority except that which God has established.

Romans 13:1

_____

_____

_____

_____

_____

_____

_____

_____

_____

_____

Trust in the Lord with all your heart and lean not on your own understanding; in all your ways acknowledge him, and he will direct your paths.

Proverbs 3:5-6

_____

_____

_____

_____

_____

_____

_____

_____

_____

I can do all things through Christ who strengthens me.

Philippians 4:13

_____

_____

_____

_____

_____

_____

_____

_____

_____

_____

_____

_____

All things work together for good to them that love God, to them who are called according to His purpose.

Romans 8:28

For God so loved the world that he gave his one and only son, that whoever believes in him shall not perish but have eternal life.

John 3:16

_____

_____

_____

_____

_____

_____

_____

_____

_____

_____

How can a young person stay pure? By obeying your word and following its rules.

Psalms 119:9

_____

_____

_____

_____

_____

_____

_____

_____

_____

_____

_____

_____

_____

Love is patient, love is kind, it does not envy it does not boast, it is not proud. It is not rude, it is not self-seeking, it is not easily angered, it keeps no record of wrong.

I Corinthian 13:4-5

_____

_____

_____

_____

_____

_____

_____

_____

_____

How great is the love the Father has lavished on us, that we should be called children of God and that is what we are.

1 John 3:1

*Fathers do not exasperate your children,
instead, bring them up in the training and
instruction of the Lord.*

Ephesians 6:4

_____

_____

_____

_____

_____

_____

_____

_____

_____

_____

Notes

Notes

Notes

Notes

_____

_____

_____

_____

_____

_____

_____

_____

_____

_____

_____

_____